Honor

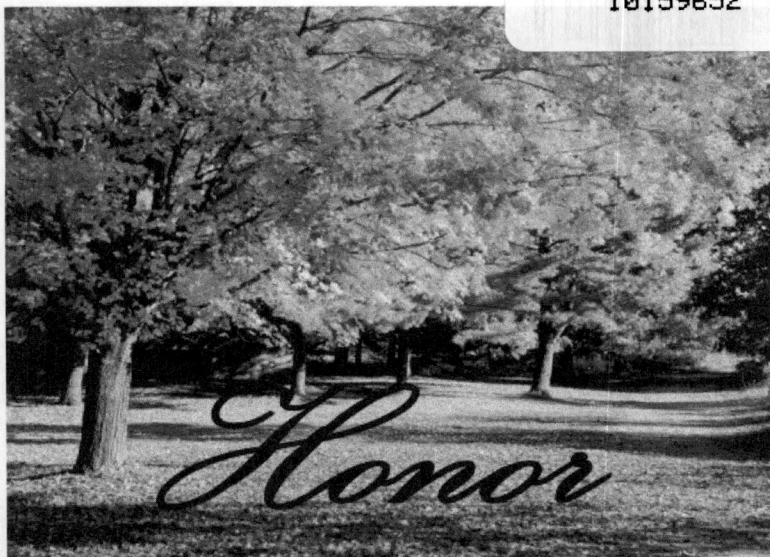

Living
a life
to
honor
your
God

Winner Torborg

Honor

"Therefore the LORD, the God of Israel, declares: 'I promised that your house and the house of your father should go in and out before me forever,' but now the LORD declares: 'Far be it from me, for those who honor me I will honor, and those who despise me shall be lightly esteemed," (1 Samuel 2:30 English Standard Version).

Bread of Life International Ministries

"Honor" by Winner Torborg

Why I use many versions of the Bible?

I do this because there is not one version that has every verse right; none of the modern versions have been translated directly from the original Hebrew, Aramaic and Greek. If I only used the King James you would get only a King James approach to God's Word; likewise, if I only used the NIV you would get an NIV approach. I wanted to share the clearest approach that I can so I must use many versions. As an ancient saying that many people claim as their own goes, "There is more than one way to go up a mountain." I use many Bibles but you must let the Holy Spirit guide you. And I suggest that you get many versions also. In one version a verse may be quoted one way and in another the same verse is quoted a totally different way.

Credentials

Almost all his life people around Winner have been trying to get the best of him. Winner was always the kind of guy who, if he found a good cause, would do he best to help. He was never one for falsity although he did have a hard time catching others in their lies.

In September of 1980, Winner Torborg made the life changing confession that Jesus is Lord; he was age of 19 years at the time. Four years later, September of 1984, at a Christian meeting Winner asked for and received the anointing of the Holy Spirit; right then everything he had read in the Bible came alive to him and his ability to learn and grasp knowledge of God's Word increased mightily. The next day he answered the call of God to step into the ministry, mainly as a teacher.

As a teacher, Winner had to learn and retain knowledge from the Bible and from watching how other people act in their lives. In September of 1985, Winner began a newsletter ministry called Bread of Life. He started by writing to a group of church people, and his ministry grew. In 1997, Winner put his ministry on the World Wide Web, and the name changed to Bread of Life International Ministries. He is now reaching people from all around the world in many different languages.

Winner also writes for many online magazines and for Bread of Life International Ministries (www.bolim.org).

Honor
Table Of Contents

Prologue

For a long time, probably as long as man has sought to honor his God, there has been one underlying question, one that underlies all others. That question is: How does one honor a God that is so supreme as Jesus? God has given me the commission to take a sincere look in the Word of God to find the truth of the matter. What I found is more than most people would think that it would take to honor God.

As with all my books, this book is not the alpha and omega of the subject; but maybe you can use this as a springboard to begin your never-ending study about the many aspects of honoring the true and living God.

When a man joins the military he is expected to honor those of higher rank than him. And he should also honor those of equal or lower rank; of course, this kind of honor must be earned.

In a business you are supposed to honor those in authority over you. But those under you must earn your honor and respect.

With God, the ruler of heaven and owner of Earth, though, it is different. With God, honor is more than an attitude of respect that can go both ways. Read this book then do your own studies. Get together with a group and do a Bible study on this subject. You will be surprised, thrilled, excited and encouraged.

Chapter 1

A Fresh Look

At the beginning of the year 2011 the Lord gave me a word for the year; this word is actually a living word to be used for all time. The word is **refresh**. He was saying, through me, not to rely on old knowledge, such as what you remember from the Bible. I used the example of Proverbs 18:21; the first time I read it was, maybe, 26 years ago, but I still get more from it every time I read it.

> "Do not conform to the pattern of this world, but be transformed by the renewing of your mind. Then you will be able to test and approve what God's will is—his good,

pleasing and perfect will," (Romans
12:2 New International Version).

Being "transformed by the renewing of
your mind" means to refresh yourself by reading
the Bible and listening to God's Word, and this
doesn't mean just once in a while. No. You
should be refreshing yourself in the Word of
God as many times as necessary; a good
measure would be at least once per day.

To mutter means to say to yourself over
and over; and many people in the world's
system tend to do that in private. Back in the
1970's and early 1980's people used to call
those who muttered to themselves where
someone else could hear, nerds. Not very nice.
By calling them names people would shame
them into not muttering to themselves. But it is
a Biblical practice to mutter to yourself, it's
called meditating on something.

"Meditate on these things;
give yourself entirely to them, that your
progress may be evident to all," 1
Timothy 4:15 New King James
Version).

Meditate is a word meaning to ponder, think on, mutter to yourself. Look at 1 Timothy 4:12-14 and see that Paul was telling the boy to dwell on what God had so graciously called him to, and not to let other people get him down.

When someone tells you something, that a Scripture means something, and you just don't see it; don't write them off declaring that he or she is wrong. This is an opportunity for you to go back the Scripture, read it again with what that person said in mind, and pray about it and that person. That person may have a point; but if you declare that they are wrong without even praying about it, you may be hurting yourself as well.

If you, when you hear a Scripture along with a meaning that *you don't like* and you **automatically** write it off as something wrong without taking a fresh look at that Scripture and praying about it, you dishonor God by saying that you know more than that person. That person may, indeed, be wrong; but your attitude is definitely wrong if you are the one doing what I just said.

Indeed, if you think he or she is wrong and you have refreshed yourself on that Scripture and prayed, in tongues and in the natural language, about it and him or her and found that he or she is in fact wrong *on all accounts*; then you can talk to that person the way 2 Timothy 2:24 says and help him or her out.

> "A servant of the Lord must not quarrel. Instead, he must be kind to everyone. He must be a good teacher. He must be willing to suffer wrong," (2 Timothy 2:24 GOD'S WORD Translation).

Brillo Pads

Look at this: I had a dirty sink and I needed something strong to clean it. I went to the store and bought some Brillo Pads. I set them on the counter; people could see them on the counter. But the sink was still dirty. I also had pots that needed to be scoured.

> "And these signs will accompany those who believe: *In my name* they will drive out demons; they

will speak in new tongues; [If] they
will pick up snakes with their hands;
and [If] when they drink deadly poison,
it will not hurt them at all; they will
place their hands on sick people, and
they will get well," (Mark 16:17-18
New International Version).

The phrase to see is underlined and in
italics and it is implied for everything
mentioned. Jesus told us that the Father will
hear us when we pray in His name,

"In that day you will no
longer ask me anything. Very truly I
tell you, my Father will give you
whatever you ask in my name, (John
16:23 New International Version).

I've gone to many Bible studies,
fellowship groups, et. al. and I have listened to
the prayers. The closing of the pray is either,
"In the name of Christ, Amen," "In the name of
Your son, Amen," "In Your name, Amen," or
"Amen." What is wrong here? Do you think
God heard or answered those prayers? The
name is Jesus; Christ is not a name; God has
many, many sons; Jesus didn't say, "In that day

you will no longer ask me anything. Very truly I tell you, my Father will give you whatever you ask in ***His name***."

Now, I had tried to clean the sink with soap and a sponge or dishcloth many times, but it never worked. I also tried the same with my pots and pans to no avail. Then I got a bit wiser and I bought some Brillo Pads. So, what if I just left them on the counter and went back to trying with the dishcloth? Suppose I was doing this to sell the house, if I sold the house would I get top dollar? After all, I have the Brillo Pads, so why aren't they working?

That's a pretty ridiculous question, but think about it: when people get the name of Jesus and put it on a pumper sticker or something, but don't use it...?

It's not hard to follow the teachings of Jesus and the plan of God, just do what Jesus said and do what Jesus did. If you do what Jesus did you will go where Jesus went (not talking about being crucified).

One time I heard a song where the person was saying, I'm trying to figure out God's will (not a quote, I don't know the exact words). God isn't dishonorable, He doesn't say one thing, even have it written down that he wants you to do it, and not want you to do what He said.

So, if you are trying to find out what God wants you to do, then the first thing you need to do is read His book (the instruction manual, the directions). Once you are firmly doing what He said to do in His directions—not letting any preacher tell you that, "This is something that only Jesus could do"—He will advance you to the next level.

Look at a video game: you don't get to the next level until you have been doing the things on the first level. Then when you get to the next level you find that you still have to do the things of the level before plus the new things of the new level. Oh, but don't worry because if you are committed to it the game master will be right there to help you.

A personal testimony: When I started out doing what God had called everyone to do it wasn't easy. But as I kept doing, it with the help of the Holy Spirit baptism, it became easier, as it seemed. Then He gave me a certain calling, and at that level things seemed hard at first, plus I had the first things to keep doing. But as I kept doing them, seemingly they got easier. Then God added another calling to my life. Again it was hard at first because now I had the first things, the second things and the third things. It was hard at first but as I kept doing them they seemed to get easier. On and on it went. It seemed hard at first, but as I kept at it and let Him work through me it became a cakewalk. I do this and God gets glory and honor from it because I do it in the name of Jesus. I'm not bragging on my abilities, but it's the name of Jesus.

Chapter 2

Committed?

I was reading a book about the positive confession the other day and I realized that the results of this confession will not take place if you only confess it once or twice and stop.

Look at an example: Jack had been speaking along the same declining ways of the world for 40 years. He felt a tickle in his throat; it made him want to cough. Well, the first thing that came to his thoughts was that he was catching a cold or something worse. So, naturally he began speaking that because he was taught in church that you have to speak it if you feel it. He went to a doctor who told him that he had a bad disease: so he began confessing that he had this disease. He did that because the doctor said that and, after all, doctors know everything about health.

When Jack was 45 he met a guy who taught him about the positive confession. So, Jack tried it once or twice and then went back to speaking and complaining about the problem. Finally, after 55 years Jack died of that bad disease.

> "Words are powerful; take them seriously. Words can be your salvation. Words can also be your damnation," (Matthew 12:37 The Message).

Where was Jack's commitment? Why didn't the positive speaking work for him? Why did he die? Was it the positive confession that killed him?

I also realized, while reading books about confession, that you tend to want what you are adamantly confessing over and over and over and over, continuously. Jack spent 40-45 years, actually 55 years, speaking the negative just like the world's system, less 2 times with the positive confession of health. Let's figure that out; let's say that each day he speaks negatively over himself once: 55 years = 20088 days, less 2. So, Jack confessed 20086 negatives over himself (must have wanted it pretty bad). But he only confessed the positive 2 times. You do the math. How much is 20088 negatives-2 positives? So, where was Jack's commitment? I'm sure, *positive*, that in 55 years Jack spoke the negative over himself more than once a day; I'd venture to say that if he was like most people he spoke negatively over himself twice – ten times each day. So, we can change that 20088 times to anywhere from 40176 times to 200880 times, minus 2 positives. Now, what's that tell you? Does the phrase, 'Elephant against a gnat' mean anything to you?

> "I can guarantee that on judgment day people will have to give an account of every careless word they say," (Matthew 12:36 GOD'S WORD Translation).
>
> "The words you say will either acquit you or condemn you," (Matthew 12:37 New Living Translation).

There used to be a phrase that my old pastor had on a pin, it said that the Word works

if you work the Word. Well, that's true but...
the Word works anyway: if you work it, it will
work for you, but if you don't work it, it will
work for the one who does. The words that you
speak work also, whether you work them for
positive or negative they will work on you.

Any time someone speaks a negative
word to you, you have a choice of responses. If
you will think, '*If I use negative words in my
response to him they will effect me negatively,
and if I use positive words they will effect me
positively,*' before you respond, you can stop a
lot of fights and ill feelings. So. before you
speak or do anything think, '*Is this what I **would
want** him to be saying or doing to me.*' You
don't have to react the way he wants you to
react; he sparked a bad reaction with his
negative words, but you don't have to react that
way. If you choose not to, and choose to give a
positive response, you can change his thoughts
and actions toward you and others.

It also shows great commitment when
you choose to respond with positive words. It
shows that you are committed when you choose
to speak positive words over yourself even
though you may look and feel terrible. It may
take until you leave this Earth for those positive
words to manifest in your life but Jesus did say

that they will work. This is a way of honoring your positive creator.

Be F.O.T.S.y

When I say be F.O.T.S.y I mean live out the fruit of the Spirit.

> "The angel said to Mary, 'The Holy Spirit will come upon you, and the power of the Most High will cover you. For this reason the baby will be holy and will be called the Son of God,'" (Luke 1:35 New Century Version).

The fruit of the Spirit is the offspring of the Spirit, which is the Son of God. So, if you are born again then you have the fruit of the Spirit in you. "Then, I have Him in me," you would say. That's good; now, live Him. "If I have Him then I am living Him." That's not necessarily so, but I hope you are.

25

See, you might know love and not be living love. It's just like a course that you took in college. When I was in college I took computer basic (a programming language), but now I couldn't put together a basic program if my life depended on it. This goes back to that old saying, a biblical saying, "Use it or loose it."

What good does it do you to have a car if you never use it? Or suppose you belong to a country club, and you have high standing with unlimited benefits. Sure, you command great respect and people there would cater to your every need whenever you were there. But what good would it do you if you slept outside the doors and acted like a vagabond? In your mansion you have a Mercedes and a Porsche, you have many rooms and millions of dollars but you do nothing with any of it because you want to be humble.

That is not being humble, that is being stupid. You could do so much good with what you have if you would only use it all.

Did you know that these aspects of the fruit of the Spirit are for you to share the life of Christ with others? They are. Sure, you can and should benefit from them; but they are not simply for your benefit. Allow me to list the fruit of the Spirit. 1) Love. That's it, that's Jesus—the fruit of the Spirit. You thought that since Galatians 5:22-23 lists nine things as the fruit of the Spirit there must be nine different fruits. No. Love is the fruit and the other eight are aspects (characteristics) of that one. Let me put it this way,

> "But the fruit of the Spirit is love, **(the characteristics of which are)** joy, peace, forbearance **(patience)**, kindness, goodness, faithfulness, gentleness and self-control. Against such things **(love and all it's characteristics in operation)** there is no law," (Galatians 5:22-23 New International Version). Words in boldface are added for purpose.

Love is a word that involves much more than just joy, peace, patience, kindness, goodness, faithfulness, gentleness and self-control. If you will, when you *make the time* to, take the English, Greek and Hebrew dictionaries *and* the thesaurus, and look up each of the eight characteristics of love, take it as far as you want. I did this to the fifth level and was pleasantly shocked; I wound up with a full 8.5 * 11 inch page of words that tied into love, either directly or indirectly.

There was a prophecy given on April 3, 2011 (it's on Youtube) about being representatives of Jesus. It explained Acts 1:8 where Jesus said that we shall be witnesses. Usually, a witness is one who saw or heard, who was there. Jesus was talking about representatives. A representative is one who has seen or heard and *does accordingly*. That's what Jesus was talking about, so let me use that word in place of **witnesses**; see if it makes sense to you.

> "But you will receive power when the Holy Spirit comes on you; and you will be my representatives in Jerusalem, and in all Judea and Samaria, and to the ends of the earth," (Acts 1:8 New International Version).

If you will represent Jesus wherever you go people will come to you. If you are doing this you don't need to do something that Jesus doesn't tell you to do; just lift up Jesus wherever you are. You are earth. You were created from the dust of the Earth.

"And I, if I be lifted up from
the earth, will draw all men unto me,"
(John 12:23 King James Version).

See, if you have joy, let joy have you;
joy will come all over you and you will radiate
joy, others will join in your joy. If peace is the
same in and on *and* about you then you will be
able to explain your peace to people who will
ask you, and they will ask you. Patience will
work peace and you will have an audience. It's
the same with all the characteristics of love and
every time you are explaining, radiating and
revealing love you are revealing Jesus. This
brings great honor and glory to God.

30

Chapter 3

Non-Stop

One reason why many people don't see the results of the positive confessing is because they give up too easily.

> "And let us not be weary in well doing: for in due season we shall reap, if we faint not," (Galatians 6:9 King James Version).

Jesus said (Luke 18:30) that if you leave something to follow Him you will reap in *this life* more than you have left. Even though Luke 18:30 is not specifically talking about the positive confession of something you prayed for, there is something from that verse that I want you to see. The 3 words, "in this life," mean sometime during your life on Earth. Now put those 3 words together with Galatians 6:9 and you have a picture of how long you need to stick with the positive confession of what you prayed for,

> "And let us not be weary in well doing: for in due season we shall reap *in this life*, if we faint not."

What does **faint** mean to you? To me it means give-up or stop or quit. The word **patience** means to be...? Calm while waiting? Yes. But it also means to be consistent, steadfast, persistent, not to faint or give-up. It is part of love, which is the fruit of the Spirit (Jesus). If you are truly born again (born of God) then you have patience.

> "Knowing this, that the trying of your faith worketh patience," (James 1:3 King James Version).

No version or translation of the Bible that I have read says that you don't have patience if you are born again; if you have Jesus in you then you have patience. But you will never realize patience—it isn't called upon to work—if there is not a trying of your faith.

So, if everything you prayed for came into manifestation instantly there would be absolutely no need for patience. Prayer would be just like a fast food chain, no waiting; no need for calmness while waiting, no need for steadfastness, consistency or persistence. The fruit of the Spirit would not include patience.

But, since patience is part of the fruit of the Spirit, and since not all prayer results manifest instantly, patience is a requirement and a factual asset. You have patience. And when you pray for something, 9.999999 times out of 10 you are going to need to use patience because your faith will be tried.

Being patient when you pray doesn't mean simply sitting by and being content that you had prayed for that thing. No, No. Being patient does not sound like a passive word to me. Though no one can see you being calm they can sure tell the difference between when you are being calm and being uptight. But being patient also means being consistent in you prayer. That doesn't mean asking consistently, but thanking consistently until the manifestation. God is steadfast in honor; you notice that He is the same always and in all ways. If you don't stop doing something that means that you are going to be persistent. You have probably heard someone who was bugged by you say, "Are you going to persist in doing that?"

So, when you begin making that positive confession according to God's Word, because of something you prayed for according to God's Word, you are going to need to use patience in all of it's meanings. Someone who prays, confesses once, then a while later confesses it again, then maybe a while later confesses it again, and gives-up because it hasn't manifested. If it does manifest it will probably be a miracle because that man, or woman, was not very persistent. "What? She said it three times," someone might argue. She fainted, she gave-up before it manifested. That means, to me, that either she decided that she didn't want it or she didn't know she had to continue until the manifestation.

In my experience, and to the best of my knowledge, those who produce great fruit that lasts are those who use patience to it's fullest. Just look at apple trees and Marigolds.

Marigolds grow one time and die, but apple trees grow over and over and produce much, much fruit. I'm not a horticulturist, but my mom used to buy marigolds every year, they would last for one season. But we used to have an apple tree in our back yard and get apples off of it every year.

> "My Father is glorified by this, that you bear much fruit, and *so* prove to be My disciples," (John 15:8 New American Standards Bible).

Read the verses around this one, Jesus was not *only* talking about making converts! So, the question is: Do you really want to honor Yahweh, the one true God? If you do then be consistent with your thankful confessions.

Pray And Call

Many people whom I have talked to seem to be against the idea of calling things that be not as though they were. One of the main reasons is because they see it as manipulating God into doing what He doesn't want to do. Well, in the first place, no one can get God to do something that He doesn't want to do; but He wants to do the things that He said that He will do in His Will.

> "If you live in Me [abide vitally united to Me] and My words remain in you and continue to live in your hearts, ask whatever you will, and it shall be done for you," (John 15:7 Amplified Bible).

This means that if you know, live, and continue to do His Will (what He said) then His Will, will become your will; call it an entwining. 1 John 5:14-15 tell us to pray according to His Will; I like to quote what is written if I can because then I know, for certain, that I am praying according to His Will.

Jesus made it quite clear that if you are doing what He wants you to do then He will answer your prayers with what you ask for.

"Very truly I tell you, whoever believes in me will do the works I have been doing, and they will do even greater things than these, because I am going to the Father. And I will do whatever you ask in my name, so that the Father may be glorified in the Son," (John 14:12-13 New International Version).

You don't see the word **maybe** anywhere in there, do you? How about the word **might**? I didn't think so. Jesus is telling you what a believer will do; then He said what He will do for the believer.

So, if you are ordering your life according to what His life said (by action)... In my spirit I just recalled a saying that I heard a long time ago, "God doesn't make robots." That's true in the fact that a robot doesn't have it's own will, we do. So, you have your own will, you can either do what Jesus said and He will answer your prays accordingly or you can go the other way.

So, if you are ordering your life, at your will, according to what His life said (by action) and what God had written is engraved in you then you can ask in prayer according to the will that is entwined with yours, your new will. Yes, it is His Will, but it is now your will.

Someone will, no doubt, argue by bringing up Matthew 7:7 and say that eastern cultures say that that means "Keep on asking, keep on seeking, keep on knocking"; indeed, the Amplified Bible says it that way. Why would you keep on knocking on a door if the person is turning the doorknob to open it? Yes, keep on asking, for new things. God doesn't mean for you not to ask for anything else. Maybe you're not just asking for your own benefit; there are plenty of people in the world who can benefit from your asking. So, if I were to ask for a new Amplified Bible, why should I keep on asking for that, He heard me; there are plenty more things to ask for in the world, not all for me but for other's who don't know Jesus yet.

And when you ask for something according to what is written He hears you and the answer is on it's way; so now, what you should be doing is honoring God by speaking as if it is already manifest.

"As it is written, I have made
you the father of many nations. [He
was appointed our father] in the sight
of God in Whom he believed, Who

gives life to the dead and speaks of the nonexistent things that [He has foretold and promised] as if they [already] existed," (Romans 4:17 Amplified Bible).

The name **Abraham** means father of a multitude, and that's what God called Abram. The man grew up with the name Abram; if there was a legal system then his name would have been on record as Abram. But God spoke things that did not appear as though they already appeared, He spoke as if Abram was already a father of many, he didn't even have one kid yet.

And Abram believed God, so he did what God did; he started calling himself Abraham before he even had one kid.

What have you prayed for according to God's Word (His

Will), according to your new will as it is entwined with God's Will? Do you see it yet, or taste it or feel it? <u>I challenge you to start speaking of that thing that you prayed for as though you have it</u>. Believe it or not, in so doing this you are giving honor to God by telling Him that you believe Him.

40

Chapter 4

Treating Yourself

"And *the* second *is* like it: *'You shall love your neighbor as yourself,'*" (Matthew 22:39 New King James Version).

How should a child of a king be treated? I've got good news for you; you are that child of a king, if you are a true Christian. Some of you are wondering, *'I'm a Christian; so, what does he mean by 'true Christian'?'* A true Christian is one who does what Jesus did (emulates The Christ); these are the true disciples of Jesus and they where called Christians at Antioch (Acts 11:26).

So, how do you treat other people? If Sodom Hussein were alive still, how would you treat him? How about Osama Bin Laden, the one called the son of Sam, John Wilks Booth, your pastor? How would you have them treat you?

> "So whatever you wish that others would do to you, do also to them, for this is the Law and the Prophets," (Matthew 11:12 English Standard Version).

This is labeled by so many as 'The Golden Rule' although many misinterpret it in the doing. Oh, they know what it says; but in the actual doing they find it most difficult to fulfill. Allow me to give an interpretation of that verse: "If you need help from others, help others. Do good to them and you will find that someone will do good to you."

You know that in order to gain friends you must show yourself friendly. I was talking to a friend a while ago who wanted to know how he could get friends. Obviously he meant friends in his town that he could do things with; I lived about 20-30 miles from him. The thing was, he made friends where I was, he just had to do the same thing in his town. So, I told him that to gain friends in his town just show himself to be a friend in his town.

A Biblical law—actually it's a natural law—says that things reproduce after their own kind. Monkeys reproduce monkeys, dogs reproduce dogs, cats reproduce cats, friends reproduce friends, help reproduces help, giving reproduces giving… But, another thing that is misunderstood about that is this. When you give or help one person you shouldn't expect that same person to give to or help you.

> "Then he turned to his host. 'When you put on a luncheon or a banquet,' he said, 'don't invite your friends, brothers, relatives, and rich neighbors. For they will invite you back, and that will be your only reward,'" (Luke 14:12 New Living Translation).

Look at Tom, Jill, Mark, Harcourt, Demetrius, Jamal, Dwayne; Mark and Tom knew each other, Demetrius hears of a rich philanthropist named Harcourt but none of the rest knew the others. Mark has a need for help working on his house but he doesn't have the money to hire a company. So, Mark asks Tom if he knows of someone who needs some furniture that he wants to give. Tom hears about a guy name Jamal who just moved to the area, and needs some furniture. So, Mark is able to give Jamal some furniture, gets to meet him and they become good friends, Mark is able to lead Jamal to Christ. Mark, Tom and Jamal get together and pray in agreement for Mark to get help working on his house. Jill comes to their church and Tom proclaims Mark's need from the pulpit; well, Jill and her husband know some carpentry, so they decide to give some help. Later on, a guy moves to the area from Naples, Italy named Demetrius and he needs everything because he had to leave everything in Naples when he left. Tom tells him about Dwayne, a guy he had just met; Dwayne had need of someone to cut his lawn and Demetrius just happened to have had, at one time, a lawn mowing business; Dwayne has a lawn mower. In a city many miles away lives a guy by the name of Harcourt, he is a millionaire inventor. Demetrius had heard of Harcourt, he heard that the man was a philanthropist who enjoyed helping needy people. Tom takes the initiative and writes to Harcourt about the needs that are prevalent in this area; so, Harcourt comes to the area to meet Demetrius, Tom and Mark, and also finds Jesus. Dwayne talks to Harcourt and tells him that he and his business will do the work on Mark and Demetrius' houses if Harcourt can supply the money. In his joy of meeting Jesus, Harcourt supplies all the money plus gives a nice sized offering to the church. This helps promote Dwayne's business and many other blessings flow.

So, who did Mark give to? Who gave to Mark?

When I was young, before I understood this principle, my parents would have dinner parties a lot. But I always knew their guests and I knew that they were all well-to-do people. The way it seemed was, it was like a tennis match where you serve to them and they send the ball back, then you send it back to them and they send it back to you. While this is okay, it's no way to grow in your community and be known as a good representative of Jesus *the* Christ; and it is also no way to help the poor.

> "Instead, invite the poor, the crippled, the lame, and the blind. Then at the resurrection of the righteous, God will reward you for inviting those

45

who could not repay you," (Luke 14:13-14 New Living Translation).

While it's fine to have your friends and neighbors to dinner, don't neglect the poor who have no one to invite them anywhere. For the most part the poor aren't invited to dinners or out to restaurants because they can't invite anyone else to dinner. Start the trend! Now, this is how The Message has Luke 14:12-14:

> "Then he turned to the host. 'The next time you put on a dinner, don't *just* invite your friends and family and rich neighbors, the kind of people who will return the favor. Invite some people who never get invited out, the misfits from the wrong side of the tracks. You'll be—and experience—a blessing. They won't be able to return the favor, but the favor will be returned —oh, how it will be returned!—at the resurrection of God's people.'"

How would you want that poor person to treat you if he could? You don't know, but that poor beggar could be an ambassador of Christ, or maybe even an angel.

"Do not neglect to show hospitality to strangers, for by this some have entertained angels without knowing it," (Hebrews 13:2 New American Standard Bible).

When you are treating others as you would have them treat you, because you love yourself as being a child of God, you are treating God the same way. Let that sink in. You are doing it as unto the Lord when you are doing it for someone else because that someone else is created by God, ultimately. So, how would you want God to treat you? No, not how has God been treating you; but how would you *want* Him to treat you? You say, "But, I'm a child of God and—" The question remains the same; how would you want Him to treat you? Whatever the answer, that is how you are going to treat others.

This is a way to honor God; by treating others as you would have others—all others—to treat you.

Treating Others

How do you treat your neighbor? How do you treat those whom you don't know? How do you treat your... self? See, Jesus says,

> "A second is equally important: 'Love your neighbor as yourself,'" (Matthew 22:39 New Living Translation).

That means that if you have self-respect then you should respect your neighbor. If you honor yourself—and there is nothing wrong with that—then honor your neighbor; that doesn't mean that you have to do everything they say without thought. If you love yourself—again, nothing wrong with a healthy self-love—then love your neighbor.

In college I met a young woman who told me, "I am a Christian. I love everyone around me but I hate myself." Well, that was evident because of all the razor scars on her wrists. But she couldn't properly love her neighbors when she hated herself. So, I had to show her that she could have a healthy love for herself; in other words, love her own life. At the end of a month she turned to me and said, "Thank you. Now I realize that I can love myself. Now I can love others." See, you can't love your neighbor unless and until you love your own life.

"For, 'Whoever would **love life** and see good days must keep their tongue from evil and their lips from deceitful speech,'" (1 Peter 3:10 New International Version).

What you do to others will always find a way to have an effect on your own live. That's why Jesus says to you,

"Do to others what you want them to do to you. This is the meaning of the law of Moses and the teaching of the prophets," (Matthew 7:12 New Century Version).

That does *not* say that *they* will do the same thing to you, but maybe someone else might. So, if you want people to hate you, hate them first. But, why would you want anyone to hate you? If you want others to curse you, well, curse others first. But why the cursing, do you want to be cursed? In the same way, do you want to be punched, maligned, treated badly, called bad names, talked badly about, called stupid? Or would you rather people call you good things, bless you, talk nice about you, help you, pray for you? Well, if you rather the later, do that to others *first*.

One day, a while ago, I had a guy come to me and say, "I just want friends. Winner, how can I get people to be my friends?" I told him that if he wanted friends what he had to do is be a friend. "Show yourself friendly, be a friend. Friends beget friends."

People used to ask me, they may still ask this question, how they can get God to be closer to them. They wanted to get close to God, but they thought that God was the One keeping His distance. James, the brother of Jesus, answered that question. He said, "Draw near to God," as in you first, "and He will draw near to you," (James 4:8).

See, God has done what he had to do. Look at this like a tennis volley. It's your serve. When you give service He responds. The more you hit the ball back, the more He hits the ball back to you. Some wise guy might say, "But He started the game with the first serve by Jesus dieing on the cross. Then we return the ball be receiving Jesus. So, now the ball is in His court." Anyway, you serve the ball and He returns it. Like I said, the more you hit it, the more He hits it. He doesn't miss. When you give it to Him He will return it.

Just so, when you start someone will return. Friends beget friends. Hatred begets hatred. Love begets love. Cursing begets cursing. Anger begets anger. Things reproduce after their own kind. It's the law of reproduction from Genesis 1:11-12. Things produce after their own kind; and they reproduce after their *own* kind.

> "Be not deceived: God is not mocked; for whatever a man shall sow, that also shall he reap," (Galatians 6:7 Darby Version).

You cannot cuss someone out and expect him or her to love you. If you go around cussing and hating everyone, don't expect anyone to love and talk nice to you. That would be dishonorable, and if you're dishonoring God and the people; only forgiveness can help you then.

Chapter 5

Not Really a Game

When I was a little kid in the back seat of my parents' station wagon and my brother was sitting next to me, he used to try to get me upset; he thought it was fun. There is a game that kids play that is supposed to get their siblings mad, it's called The Copy-Cat Game. Many of you know it, you've probably even taken part in it; it's a game to you when you are doing it to annoy your little brother or sister. Everything he or she would say, you would say; when he or she would complain to your mom that you were copying him or her, you would say the same thing. This annoyed them to no end; but you thought it was so funny. Of course, neither of you knew Jesus at the time.

Well, now that you are born again you think of that Copy-Cat Game as just a game; some of you might even remember doing it to your sibling and cringe at the hurt you caused them. Now, look at something that the Apostle Paul said,

> "Be imitators of me, just as I also am of Christ," (1 Corinthians 11:1 New American Standard Bible).

Paul was telling the people, of which you are one, to be a copycat of him as long as he was a copycat of Jesus, who is the Christ. Paul was a representative of the Christ, so he had to be anointed just like Jesus. He imitated Jesus because he had the same anointing, the Holy Spirit.

Jesus is the big brother of those who are born again, and God is the Father. Now, Jesus says to you,

> "So Jesus explained, "I tell you the truth, the Son can do nothing by himself. He does only what he sees the Father doing. Whatever the Father does, the Son

also does," (John 5:19 New Living
Translation).

Jesus said that He copies His Father.
Now how can He tell you to *just* sit in the
church pew and listen or watch? No! You who
are born of God are representatives *in kind* of
Jesus; that means that you are called to be a
Jesus to the world. Remember what Jesus said
when the Greek men wanted to see Him,

> "I assure you, most solemnly
> I tell you, Unless a grain of wheat falls
> into the earth and dies, it remains [just
> one grain; it never becomes more but
> lives] by itself alone. But if it dies, it
> produces many others and yields a rich
> harvest," (John 12:24 Amplified Bible).

That was definitely a figure of speech
meaning that after Jesus went to the grave and
rose He would be in those who would receive
Him. Therefore, if you have received Him *and
given your life to God*, you are Jesus in kind, as
a representative. But Jesus' representatives are
not *just* supposed to do what Jesus did by action
(John 14:12). No, Jesus also said,

55

"This is true, because I have not spoken on my own authority, but the Father who sent me has commanded me what I must say and speak," (John 12:49 Good News Translation).

Jesus spoke and speaks what the Father tells Him to speak and He wants you to do the copycat thing to Him; in other words say what he says and do what He does.

I go around and listen to some Christians speak—they don't know I'm there—and I think, *Would Jesus say that?* These people that I heard talking negatively have a key ring or neck-strap or something that has that popular slogan W.W.J.D. Obviously, they don't know what Jesus would do, because they aren't doing it. That, or they are false themselves and don't care.

Do you really and truly want to honor God? Do the copycat thing and make Him your target; do what He would do in… how many situations? Well, how much do you want to show honor to your God? How far do you want to go in honoring God; all the way, part way, or what? You see, when you honor God, He honors you. So, if you want to go all the way in honoring God then do what He does in all things.

Things Are

Firewood is $5 for five sticks. That is very high, especially considering that trees grow free. But instead of people confessing that firewood prices are coming down they confess that the prices are high and getting higher. Of course, you know that I'm only using this as an example; I don't know what the price of firewood is.

Christians want to honor God; I do and I would hope that you do too. If you will read John 14:12 carefully... Let me quote it,

> "Very truly I tell you, whoever <u>believes</u> in me <u>will do</u> the works I have been doing, and they will do even greater things than these, because I am going to the Father,"

(John 14:12 New International Version).

Notice the three words that I underlined, believes, will do. That tells me that if I believe —the Amplified Bible says steadfastly believe (constantly believe)—I will copy the one whom I believe. Let me ask you; does God ever speak negatively over anything concerning you? Such as your health; does God ever tell you that you are deathly sick? Or about your finances; does God ever tell you that you are going broke?

God called Abram a father of a multitude, that's what **Abraham** means. Abram believed God, so what did he do? Did he say, "Well, yea, God said I am a father of many, but I don't even have one kid yet."? No. He understood that to really believe is to do the same as, to copy; this honors the person you believe. So, Abram started calling himself Abraham, meaning father of a multitude. Don't you know that those who heard him thought he was nuts when he said, "God called me a father of many so I am a father of many." Remember, when he was saying this he had no children at all. Sounds goofy, doesn't it?

Now look at Jacob, the man who was called a usurper, he seemed to live up to his name. At Laban's house he used his scheming ways, but so did Laban. If he were alive today he would probably be in jail, or at least an untrustworthy outcast. But, look at what happened,

> "And he said, Thy name shall be called no more Jacob, but Israel: for as a prince hast thou power with God and with men, and hast prevailed," (Genesis 32:28 King James Version).

<u>As a prince hast thou power with God and with men</u>. So, what do you think the man called himself after that? Did he call himself Jacob, or Israel?

Okay, now look in the New Testament at Simon Bar Jonah (his name was not Simon Peter). Simon was a loud-mouthed fisherman who seemed to like being first. He was not a rock, but a leaf blowing in the wind. This is what happened; when Jesus and His crew were in Caesarea Philipi they sat down for lunch somewhere, probably just Jesus and His twelve. (Taken from Matthew 16:13-18). Jesus asked them; "Who do people say that the Son of Man is?" His twelve answered with what they had heard from the people who hung around them most of the time. But then Jesus asked the twelve, "Who do you say that the Son of Man is?" Simon took the queue as the spokesman of the crew, or maybe it was just him that got it, and he said, "You are the Christ, God's Son." This knowledge wasn't given to him by man, it was a revelation from God (it may have come to the whole crew, I don't know).

Peter means firm, unwavering, as in not blown about by every wind of doctrine. And the man had to grow into that name; he wasn't firm when the name was given to him. Israel wasn't ready to rule as God when his name was given to him. Abraham didn't even have one child when his name was given to him. So, why do you have to see it in manifestation, apparent, before you will say that it's there?

> "As it is written: 'I have made you a father of many nations.' He is our father in the sight of God, in whom he believed—the God who gives life to the dead and calls into being things that were not," (Romans 4:17 New International Version).

Now, I have heard what many *so-called* Christians have been saying about the economy, gas prices, their own health, their own finances, their president, their car, their neighbors, whatever. These people would feel something wrong, hear bad news from their doctor or the news media, see gas prices rise, loose some money on something, or whatever. And their words propel the rising prices, which they don't like, their words propel the lose of money, which they don't like, their words propel any negative news from the news media or the doctor, which they don't like, their words propel sickness, which they don't like. Can you sense a pattern?

Why do you think that gas prices are going the direction that they are going? Someone down the line started the ball rolling by communicating the rise; it would only make sense that it started with words. Personally, I had prayed and I have been confessing gas prices to come down. People would say I'm crazy for doing so, but if everyone were to be doing the same thing it would happen. After all, I am one man confessing that they are coming down. How many are confessing the opposite, just because that's what they see, even though they don't like it?

Do you think that God would start confessing the negative just because that is what the signs suggest? Is that something that you would imagine Jesus doing? Do you think that by confessing the negative just because that's what the signs suggest would be honoring God? So, why are you doing it, confessing that prices are rising, confessing that you are sick—dieing, confessing disasters, confessing broken car and all that trash if that's not honoring God?

Do you want to honor God? Do you believe God? Will you do what God did and does? Pray about this and honor God by doing and saying what He does and says. Jesus is God in the flesh and so are you, you who are truly *Christ*ian-anointed men and women of God.

Chapter 6

Why Was The Bible Written?

Is the Bible a history book, as some have thought of it? Well, it does have some qualities of a historical account in it, a history of the Jewish nation. But, this historical account ended millennia ago and then it doesn't cover very much of the Jewish race; only 1 or 2 people for each regime. The Bible tells a history of God's intervention in the lives of a certain line of people from the beginning.

This history begins with God's creation of the physical foundations of the Earth, trees and vegetation, animals and Earth creatures and sea creatures, and the beginnings of mankind. The second step to this history was following not all people but one line of people; those who were called Hebrews. At times it would seem that the Bible jumped to the life story of different races, but later we find out that these foreigners had a part to play in the birth of the Son of God.

But then, when we get to the books of the prophets the Bible is not just history anymore; it becomes a 'foretelling book.' Prophecies are not history; they are for telling the outcome and what God is going to do. Most of these prophecies were foretelling the life of Jesus, the Son of God.

Then we get to the point in the Bible that most people call the New Testament. The first four books of the New Testament are an account of the ministry of Jesus; how Jesus started His ministry by first being baptized in water, then in the Holy Spirit; how Jesus was tested in the wilderness as a preparation; and his actions. Then Jesus was crucified, which is what some believe is the point where the Old Testament truly ends.

Then comes the book of Acts, the acts of the Holy Spirit through those who believe and receive Him. This is the book written about the acts of the Church of Jesus; these people, not only believed and confessed that Jesus is

Lord, meaning the One whom they were going to obey, but continued to obey Him in word and actions.

Then we have the letters to the people of the Church who were in foreign lands, telling them basic things that they need to watch for and continue doing.

Finally we have a book called *The Revelation*, which tells about the end of times.

Why Was The Bible Written? Part 2

Now, most people, when they get born again by confessing that Jesus is Lord, are taught that they have done what it takes to get to heaven and that whenever Jesus comes back to get His own they will go with Him. Well, in that case the Bible didn't have to be written and passed down to you; only this 1 verse needed to be written,

"If you confess with your mouth that Jesus is Lord and believe in your heart that God raised him from the dead, you will be saved," (Romans 10:9 New Living Translation).

The first four books of what you call the New Testament are not only descriptive books about Jesus' ministry, but they are also instructional books telling you how to live as one of God's own children (believers in Jesus). Jesus, Himself, said,

"I tell you the truth, anyone who believes in me will do the same works I have done, and even greater works, because I am going to be with the Father," (John 14:12 New Living Translation).

I believe that if a person wants to find the definition of a Biblical word, such as the word **believe,** that person should look in the Bible. In the Bible there are definitions of the word **believe**. Here Jesus used the word in conjunction with the phrase **will do**. Notice what He said, "…anyone who believes in me will do…"

If you knew your natural father and your big brother loved you dearly, and you loved them and believed them; do you think that they would tell you to do something that would hurt you? If you knew it would please them if you did it; would you do it? What if you knew that your brother told you that if you did it then he would do something for you? Well now, take a look at the next verse,

> "You can ask for anything in my name, and I will do it, so that the Son can bring glory to the Father," (John 14:13 New Living Translation).

So, just because you decided that Jesus is Lord doesn't mean that you have arrived at the airport and you have your ticket to fly, destination heaven; not unless you were to die at that very instant of confession. No! What you did when you confessed your faith in Jesus being Lord was declare whom you are going to obey. You just purchased your ticket and now you have to obey the road map on that ticket to go to that special airport. The journey to the airport is called the life of a true Christian, living Christ in your life. The Bible contains that ticket.

Many of Jesus' disciples teach the baptism in the Holy Spirit as part of being obedient to His commands; that is called giving yourself to God or strengthening your commitment to Jesus. When a person lays hands on the sick, casts out a demon, or speaks in other tongues, it is God's Holy Spirit doing the work through that person; the person is simply allowing God to use his or her body.

Chapter 7

Tithes And Offerings

Did Jesus tithe? There is nothing written about this matter in the four Gospels, or anywhere else in the Bible either. However, Jesus didn't break any law or go against His Father in any way.

> "Do not think that I have come to abolish the Law or the Prophets; I have not come to abolish them but to fulfill them," (Matthew 5:17 New International Version).

Tithing was not a commandment in the written code of the Ten Commandments, but Tithing (giving the first tenth) was practiced all through the Bible as an ordinance of believers as thanksgiving to the One who gave them the rights over the property. God gave the believers the property and, out of honor, respect and gratitude, the believer gave the tithe back to God.

> "And all the tithe of the land, whether of the seed of the land, or of the fruit of the tree, is the LORD's: it is holy unto the LORD," (Leviticus 27:30 King James Version).

Yes, you're right, it was something that God required us to observe. And, being an upright man, there should be no doubt in your mind that Joseph taught the tithe to his family. He tithed, himself, and his whole family, of which Jesus was a part, was a tithing family.

Now, should you tithe? If you love, honor and respect (the fear of the Lord) God then yes, by all means. Some people hold back their tithe because they 'run out of money before they run out of month.' But, don't worry about that; if you set yourself to be a habitual tither (you're going to tithe first no matter what) then God will honor your persistence and get the money to you.

Testimony time: Back when I was first Holy Spirit baptized I made up my mind to be a tither. When I fell ill and lost my job I stuck with the tithe, even though I was hardly making a dime. But other people, people whom I didn't know but whom God put in my way, paid my bills for me. Because of an operation I was put on welfare, making about $200 each month. But I continued to tithe and God continued to take care of me. Soon welfare handed my case to social security and supplemental security income because they couldn't afford me anymore, and my financial standing rose; God still had those people paying my bills. My dad had already told me that He was done paying for my college or my housing. When I moved to Tulsa, Oklahoma my bills didn't come for the first two months, but neither did my checks. When the checks came they were just enough for my rent; but I had already committed to the tithe. So, I tithed even though that left me without enough for the rent. Before the rent was due my dad, who had already told me that he wouldn't pay my rent, called and said that he was going to pay my rent; I never asked him. Now I own my own house and am doing a lot better, financially, and it is all because of my persistence to tithe even when tithing would mean that I might have to depend on God to get my bills paid.

Here are some of the benefits of being a tither:

> "Bring the whole tithe into the storehouse, that there may be food in my house. Test me in this," says the LORD Almighty, "and see if I will not throw open the floodgates of heaven and pour out so much blessing that there will not be room enough to store it, (Malachi 3:10 New International Version).

So I am adamant about the tithe because it brings joy, honor and glory to God, and to me it brings joy. But that doesn't mean that I can be foolish with the rest of my money. No. If I had an income $1000 and I owe $1000 on bills I would still tithe $100 and come out with $900. But I would put that $900 for my bills and not buy stuff that I don't *need*, really desperately need, until God came through and I paid all my bills.

Now for the offerings. They are separate from the tithe; but this is what God said to the Jews who were robbing God, when they asked Him;

> "Will a man rob God? Yet you are robbing Me! But you say, 'How have we robbed You?' In tithes and offerings," (Malachi 3:8 New American Standard Bible).

You will notice the last three words, **tithes** *and* **offerings.** That means that withholding offerings is also a dishonor to God. You might be a tither, totally committed to the tithe, but not do any giving apart from the first tenth. Because you tithe you think that you are safe from a curse (read the next verse). Do you know what that word, **and**, means? That means tithes plus offerings; n other words it's not a full sign of love honor and respect to tithe and hold back on offerings.

Two things about offerings that make them different from the tithe: Offerings can be any amount, after you tithe of course; a tithe is set at ten percent of your income, and offerings can go directly to the poor, to a Christian organization, or to the church, the tithe goes to the local church where you get your spiritual food.

73

"Each of you should give what you have decided in your heart to give, not reluctantly or under compulsion, for God loves a cheerful giver," (2 Corinthians 9:7 New International Version).

Personally, I consider Jesus as my heart; so when Paul wrote that we should give as we purposed in our heart I take it that I should talk to Jesus and give as He directs. And for some who might be afraid to do that He doesn't always ask you to give everything; unless keeping it would wind you up in a prideful situation or sin.

Because of what Malachi 3:8 says I do believe that Jesus was a giver also, He gave offerings. There were plenty of poor in Israel then and plenty of people, organizations I'm sure, set up to help them. And I'm sure that Jesus, either directly from Jesus or through Judas or Matthew (the money bag holder), gave.

So, if you're giving tithes and offerings, that's terrific. This is part of the way of honoring God? It is not the only way, but it most definitely is one way, a part of the way. It is definitely a good way of showing God that

74

you recognize where the money and supplies are coming from. The money might comes through you job or social security or wherever; they are not sources, but only channels. Just like the water doesn't come from the river, but through the river; it comes from the ocean. God is the source of all goodness and He sends it through your job or wherever or whomever.

I'm sure you have probably heard the story about priming the pump. Priming the pump means putting water down a water pump so that you can draw more water out. Cattle ranchers, at least from the days before plumbing, know this. They would get water from the pump to water their cattle and themselves, and then they would fill a jar with some extra water. The extra water was to prime the old pump so that they could get water again to water their cattle and themselves again. And the process would continue.

Well giving the tithe and offering is, sort of, like priming the pump. When you get your provision out you save a portion. But you don't hold that portion until the next time; you put it back right then. And because you had put that portion back already the pump is already primed.

So, should you tithe? Well, I certainly would if I were you. I can't make you do anything that you don't want to do. But, knowing that giving you tithes and offerings is a way to show God that you love, honor and respect Him and that you recognize Him as the source of all the goodness in your life. To be sure, doing this brings joy to His heart, so it should probably be the first physical thing that you do; well, besides praising Him of course.

> "Still, you did well by sharing with me in my hardship, (4:14 Holman Christian Standard Bible), Moreover, as you Philippians know, in the early days of your acquaintance with the gospel, when I set out from Macedonia, not one church shared with me in the matter of giving and receiving, except you only; for even when I was in Thessalonica, you sent me aid more than once when I was in need. Not that I desire your gifts; what I desire is that more be credited to your account, (4:15-17 New International Version), At the moment I have all I need—and more! I am generously supplied with the gifts you sent me with Epaphroditus. They are a sweet-

smelling sacrifice that is acceptable and pleasing to God, (4:18 New Living Translation), *And* my God will meet all your needs according to the riches of his glory in Christ Jesus," (4:19 New International Version). (Philippians 4:14-19).

Remember, **and** is an addition word; They meaning for the **and** in verse 19 is that Paul adds verse 19 onto verse 18, which groups it with verses 14-17.

Chapter 8

Hands On

Jesus laid hands on the sick and the sick recovered, instantly as recorded. You may have noticed that Jesus never prayed, "Father, please heal this person." Some would say, "Well, that's because He was God on Earth." It's true that Jesus was God on Earth. But all those people take that argument as a reason why they can't lay hands on the sick for recovery seem to overlook something that the apostle Paul realized. Let's look in Philippians.

> "Although he was in the form of God and equal with God, he did not take advantage of this equality. Instead, he emptied himself by taking on the form of a servant, by becoming like other humans, by having a human

appearance," (Philippians 2:6-7 GOD'S WORD Translation).

According to those verses, Jesus did everything that He did on Earth as a man under the Abrahamic covenant. The good news is that if He did those things that He did as a man with a covenant with God, then as men under the same covenant (the covenant refreshed and new) we can do the same.

Authority

When God created mankind He gave them authority to rule the earth. Someone undoubtedly will argue, "No he didn't. He gave us dominion." A synonym of **dominion** is **authority**. Yes, I do know that satan came in and stole that authority by deception, the fall of man. When Jesus came and died for man, defeated the devil *on his own turf*, then was raised from the dead, He told His disciples,

> "Then Jesus came to them and said, 'All authority in heaven and on earth has been given to me,'"

(Matthew 28:18 New International
Version).

Yes, but what was Jesus going to do
with that authority? He didn't need authority on
Earth unless He was going to stay on Earth as
one physical man. Check out the next verse,

> "Therefore go and make
> disciples of all nations, baptizing them
> in the name of the Father and of the
> Son and of the Holy Spirit," (Matthew
> 28:19 New International Version).

There is an implied phrase that Jesus
said, it's not written in the translation but
implied. If He were to send us out to make
disciples without giving us authority He would
be doing us an injustice. So, what is the implied
statement? How did Jesus give us the authority
to do everything that we need to do? He gave us
His name, gave us power of attorney. The name
of Jesus is the name of authority. Jesus had
authority over the weather—He calmed the
storm—He had authority over demons and over
sickness. He even had authority over the beasts
of the field. How do I know?

81

"And God said, Let us make man in our image, after our likeness: and let them have **dominion** over the fish of the sea, and over the fowl of the air, and over the cattle, and over all the earth, and over every creeping thing that creepeth upon the earth," (Genesis 1:26 King James Version).

If God gave it to mankind when He created him then Jesus took it back from satan when He took all authority back. Then Jesus gave all the authority that God originally gave us back to us. Plus, Jesus said that we, believers, would do what He did,

"I tell you the truth, anyone who believes in me will do the same works I have done, and even greater works, because I am going to be with the Father," (John 14:12 New Living Translation).

If Jesus did it and we have the opportunity to do it also, we should do it because we can and He would want us to. Did Jesus calm storms? There were plenty of wild beasts in that area then; do you think He let them hurt Him or His friends? There was plenty of demonic activity there, then; do you think He coward under that oppression? There was plenty of disease there in that time; do you think He took any of that nonsense or even allow it to bother His people? What did He do?

And when he came back from the grave, back from hell, He gave us all the same authority. He honored His Father by using the authority that God had given Him. Jesus never lost His authority; it was us, you and me, who lost our authority. But, now that Jesus took back our authority from the bad guy and gave it back to us, the authority that God gave us in the beginning; are you going to honor your Father, God, by using that authority?

There is one thing that is conspicuous in its absence about the authority that God gave mankind. Look, again, at Genesis 1:26; we, you and I, have authority-dominion over fish, birds, animals, and insects *and* over the Earth itself. Jesus added to our authority by giving us authority over the weather, demons, and sickness, *and* our *own* lives. Do you honor Jesus and the Father? Then walk in and operate in your authority. One major way to do this is by your words.

83

Chapter 9

Why Plant Weeds?

> "Then he told them many things in parables, saying: 'A farmer went out to sow his seed,'" (Matthew 13:3 New International Version).
>
> "When anyone hears the message about the kingdom and does not understand it, the evil one comes and snatches away what was sown in their heart. This is the seed sown along the path," (Matthew 13:19 New International Version).

Here you can see that the Word concerning the Kingdom of God is a seed. Actually any word is a seed, whether for good or bad. Good seeds make for good fruit (results); bad seeds make for bad fruit (results).

I talked to a friend who is a farmer and knows about planting and harvesting. This is what I had thought about; when planting weeds ten miles away they will, eventually, get back to you, so I asked him about it. He confirmed what I had thought. When a farmer plants corn or wheat or soybeans or whatever he plants one seed and harvests one plant (of course, he doesn't just plant one seed, but many). But then someone who hates him sneaks around and throws a seed of a weed in his crop. It might depend upon what kind of weed it is but the weed may or may not spring up fast. But either way the roots of the weed go deep. And what's more is that they will spread out in many directions, including the direction of the rascal who through that seed in his field. Let's see if I can draw you a picture.

corn   the weed

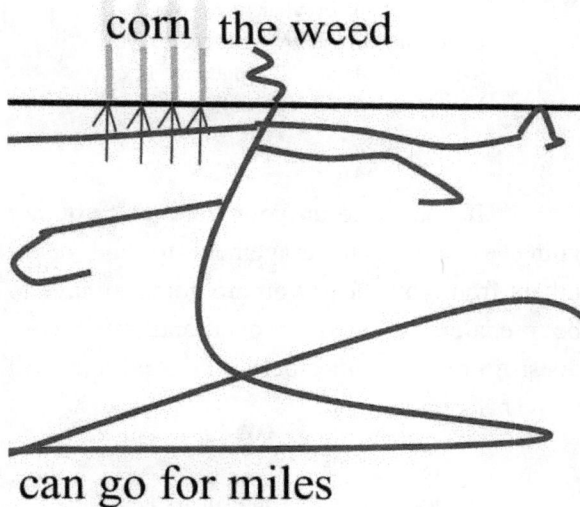

can go for miles

If you speak a bad, insulting, cursing, detrimental, death oriented word to someone or about someone you are planting a weed in his or her field. And, since those roots get back to you, eventually, in effect you are speaking them over yourself. And, since you spoke (planted) them somewhere else you will not be able to dig them up when they get back to you. The best thing for you to do is to think before you speak. So they made you mad by doing a foolish thing, so what! You can condemn yourself by your words, if you really want to; but you have no right to condemn them by your words.

87

"For by your words you will be acquitted, and by your words you will be condemned," (Matthew 12:37 New International Version).

If you make up your mind that you are going to speak encouragement to and about others from your heart you are going to have to be prepared to speak it over and over; corn doesn't grow ten times per seed. And they will come back on you too.

"Give, and it shall be given unto you; good measure, pressed down, and shaken together, and running over, shall men give into your bosom. For with the same measure that ye mete withal it shall be measured to you again," (Luke 6:38 King James Version).

But, if you make up your mind that, *'That guy really hurt me...,'* by a stupid mistake, *'so I'm gonna hurt him.'* And you say just one bad thing about him, then you had better repent fast and apologize because if you don't, *right away*, then Matthew 12:37 is happening. Satan will take advantage of, even, one bad word.

And, why plant weeds in your own field? Just because the doctor finds something that he thinks is wrong doesn't mean that you must agree with him and speak the same thing. When a person goes to a doctor that person thinks that doctor is the one whom he should believe (speak the same as) and agree with. So, why would you rather believe the doctor's fallible report and begin confessing along with it rather than believe God's infallible report and begin confessing along with it?

What does God say about you? What does God say about that person who hurt you? What do you say about you? What do you say about that person who hurt you?

Remember, your words will, eventually, get back to you and have an effect on your life; you are also God's. So, do your words, what you just said and what you usually say, honor God?

Actions

People have adopted the line, "Actions speak louder than words." Now, I ask you: is that true at all times and for everyone? It is most definitely true for the person who cannot talk; but it is not true for people who can. It is used as an excuse for those who want to do good but don't want to speak right. See, in Matthew 12:37 Jesus is not talking about your works, but about your words. Look carefully at this Scripture:

> "You brood of vipers, how can you who are evil say anything good? For the mouth speaks what the heart is full of. A good man brings good things out of the good stored up in him, and an evil man brings evil things out of the evil stored up in him. But I tell you that everyone will have to give account on the day of judgment for every empty word they have spoken. For by your words you will be acquitted, and by your words you will be condemned," (Matthew 12:34-37 New International Version).

For a minute I want you to look at that Scripture, again, and take the word **empty** out; read it out loud and slowly. That day of judgment is the day when your words manifest in your live. I write those words from personal experience and from Biblical deductive reasoning. Jesus said that if a man leaves; **leaves** covers any type of departing from; he shall receive *in this lifetime*. If you leave your words, or a better way of looking at that, if your words leave you they will come back and manifest in your life sometime during your lifetime. Jesus never said that the manifestation of your words will be at the end of your life, but in your lifetime.

So, you won't know when the judgment-manifestation day will be, but it will be in your lifetime. It could be one second before you depart this life but you don't know. For instance: My old pastor had cancer. He claimed his healing and was healed; but the manifestation came one second before he went to heaven, healthy. So, when people tell you to watch what you say they are telling you that your words are going to come back on you and you really don't want bad words to come back on you. Although, they should not jump on your case; they should teach you gently.

Then people will tell you that you will be judged for the works that you have done while on Earth. Well,

"And I saw a great white throne, and him that sat on it, from whose face the earth and the heaven fled away; and there was found no place for them. And I saw the dead, small and great, stand before God; and the books were opened: and another book was opened, which is the book of life: and the dead were judged out of those things which were written in the books, according to their works. And the sea gave up the dead which were in it; and death and hell delivered up the dead which were in them: and they were judged every man according to their works," (Revelation 20:11-13 King James Version).

That passage of Scripture was written about the time after the thousand-year reign, which is a thousand years after the end of the world as we know it. Now, I said that *we*, too, will be judged for *our* works. Which works are they?

"Truly, truly, I say to you, whoever believes in me will also do the works that I do; and greater works than these will he do, because I am going to the Father," (John 14:12 English Standard Version).

You're going to be judged, and I am going to be judged, for both; our words and the works that we do *as a believer in Jesus*, and those works are the works that He does, plus the greater works. Now, what are the greater works? Well, after you have been doing what Jesus does He will add to you a special calling, or 2 or 3 or however many you can handle. He knows what you can handle and He will not give you more than you can handle.

"So any person who knows what is right to do but does not do it, to him it is sin," (James 4:17 Amplified Bible).

There is a popular emblem, "W.W.J.D." meaning what would Jesus do. But many of the people who wear that emblem are not doing what Jesus would do. If you are going to ask what Jesus would do in any particular situation, you had better be prepared to do it. I say that because if you ask you are going to get the answer, if you are sincere in your asking. And if you get the answer then you will know the right thing to do. So, if you don't do it, to you it is a sin; you have just sinned in your own sight. Therefore, the emblem or phrase should be, "Do as Jesus would do."

Your actions should line up with your words, and your words should line up with God's Word. So, if you decide that your "actions speak louder than words," you are telling me that you want to continue lying; if your words are not lined up with God's Word, which is truth, at the precise moment, then you are lying; that is if your actions and your word disagree. People, this is not honorable and it dishonors God.

Do your actions honor God, or do they honor your religious ideas? If you find, after doing some soul-searching, that you are not honoring God, totally, with your actions *and* words then repent and turn toward the right.

Chapter 10

Do You Really Love The Lord?

"Those who know my commands and obey them are the ones who love me, and my Father will love those who love me. I will love them and will show myself to them," (John 14:21 New Century Version).

Jesus was saying, and is saying now, that those who truly love Him do what He says. He did what He said; He said "Lay hands on the sick" and He healed by the laying on of hands or by some other means that the recipient chose; He said "Cast out demons" and He cast out demons. He told us to do it because the Father told Him to do it, and He did it too.

Christians always say that Jesus was our substitute. He was our substitute in death; but, unfortunately, many take Him as our substitute in everything (He did it so we don't have to, or He can do it but we can't). Jesus *was* our substitute in death; He died spiritually so that we don't have to. But in doing things, obeying His commands, doing like Him, He *is* our standard or pattern. We are supposed to pattern our lives (lives of obedient action) after His life of obedient action.

> "Verily, verily, I say unto you, He that believeth on me, the works that I do shall he do also; and greater works than these shall he do; because I go unto my Father," (John 14:12 King James version).

Allow me to take John 14:12 and John 14:21, smash them together and paraphrase, with the Lord's permission. "With the greatest sincerity I tell you that he who believes in me and loves me more than any other will keep my commands as I do and will copy me as I do them. My Father and I will love him and I will show myself to him, and then he will do even greater works because I am with the Father."

Am I writing these things to make you feel like a slave who has no rights? No! In fact, the verses right after John 14:12 says this,

"And I will do [I Myself will grant] whatever you ask in My Name [as presenting all that I AM], so that the Father may be glorified and extolled in (through) the Son," (Amplified Bible).

That **and** means that if you are doing the previous verse then He is going to keep His word to you and do what you ask. Fact is that there are other verses that say that Jesus/God will do something for you *if* you will do His Word; just off the top of my head there is John 15:7, John 16:21, 1 John 5:14-15, and Mark 11:22-25. These all go together. Truly, the message of Jesus is all talking about one main thing. He wants you to do what He says then He will do what He told you that He would for you. Sure, there are other small sub-messages. But, you have no right to expect Him to answer your requests if you aren't obeying His Word.

You can very easily see how honor comes into this. If you can't, let me help you.

One synonym of **honor** is respect, which is the same as reverence. How is it possible for anyone to love Jesus and call Him Lord and not respect Him? If someone claims to love Jesus and has no respect or reverence for Him they are lying, blatantly. So, the one who is going to love Jesus must (seriously must) honor, respect and reverence Him; that means reverently fear Him.

Okay, take John 14:21 and the paraphrase I gave (the paraphrase of John 14:21 and 14:12) and replace all instances of the word **love** with the word **honor**. Read along *and out loud*; "With the greatest sincerity I tell you that he who believes in me and honors me more than any other will keep my commands as I do and will copy me as I do them. My Father and I will honor him and I will show myself to him, and then he will do even greater works because I am with the Father."

True Love

If you ask any person who calls himself or herself a Christian if they rally love Jesus they would answer yes. Many of them do things that *they* consider obedience; they go to foreign soil and take part in passing out food, they go to nursing homes and sing to the elderly, they work in soup kitchens and help out in homeless shelters. And they will tell you that they feel compelled to do this because of the love of God, because they love Jesus. But, is it because they truly love-honestly believe Jesus or because they want to be thought of as true followers of Jesus?

I just read a Scripture the other day, one that I have read so many times before, and read 2 verses in it that spoke volumes to me. The Scripture is Mark 11:12-25, and the specific verses are verses 13-14,

> "Seeing in the distance a fig tree in leaf, he went to find out if it had any fruit. When he reached it, he found nothing but leaves, because it was not the season for figs. Then he said to the tree, 'May no one ever eat fruit from you again.' And his disciples heard him say it," (New International Version).

I wondered about this, so I asked about it. See, this fig tree represents many people who call themselves Christians and want others to see them as Christians also. They make a show of being a good Christian; they are full leafy trees. But the fruit is for God to eat; it's the fruit of Jesus working through you.

There are people who love you and *say* that they would die for you, and *maybe* they would. But, do they do what you do? Do they believe what you believe? Think about this: Do you believe what Jesus believes? Do you do what Jesus does? Would you die, physically, for Jesus? Would you *voluntarily* suffer pain for Him?

One day a radio hostess said something like, have you given you live to Christ. That made me think because we get born again by confessing Jesus as Lord. Many people who call themselves Christians think they are saved because they have confessed Jesus as Lord; but Scripture says,

> "that if you confess with your
> mouth Jesus *as* Lord, and believe in
> your heart that God raised Him from
> the dead, you will be saved;" (Romans
> 10:9 New American Standard Bible).

That says to me that if you do that you will be—in line to—be saved, or will as in future possibilities. Your future is not written yet, you write it every day. But she was saying give your life to Him, not accept Him or His life. There is a difference. The difference is that when one accepts Jesus he is a fan; and, although he might think that he's doing things for Jesus, he is actually doing them for himself, to look leafy, to look like he is doing 'the Christian thing.' But *after* accepting Jesus and God's way for you, if you give your life to Him (get baptized in His Holy Spirit) He can use your life and make His presence known through, in *and on* you.

Smith Wigglesworth was Holy Spirit baptized. One time while he was on a train he walked past a Catholic priest who fell on the floor convicted of sin. Smith hadn't even opened his mouth. It was God's presence made known on Smith.

Do you want to honor God? Then don't just be a leafy fig tree, trying to make everyone think that you are a Christians, going places and doing things to make yourself and others feel good about you. Give your life to God and be baptized in His Spirit; and let Him make His presence known through, in and on you. Allow

Him full access to you, every square inch of your whole life.

When Jesus was asked what the greatest commandment was He said,

> "The most important one," answered Jesus, "is this: 'Hear, O Israel: The Lord our God, the Lord is one. Love the Lord your God with all your heart and with all your soul and with all your mind and with all your strength.'" (Mark 12:29-30 New International Version).

In other words; love Him with everything you are, and give Him everything you are and everything you have. That doesn't mean that you have to give up your house, your car, all your money, whatever. But, if He asks you for it you should do it.

Chapter 11

The Denominational Barriers

Many years ago I was given a ride to church. Since the word **church** signified to the driver that I am Christian I was asked what denomination I am. I looked straight at the driver and said, "I'm not denominated, I'm of the numerator. And that is Jesus."

Look at this fraction for a minute, 1/25. Which is the numerator and which is the denominator? Well, it's the same in the Church; the body is one and that is the numerator. Now, if Christ is the numerator, which He is, then the denominator-denominations-is what changes. I know that in mathematics it is the numerator that changes as you add, but... That's what denominations do; they put God in a box.

"My brothers, some from Chloe's household have informed me that there are quarrels among you. What I mean is this: One of you says, 'I follow Paul; another, 'I follow Apollos'; another, 'I follow Cephas'; still another, 'I follow Christ.' Is Christ divided? Was Paul crucified for you? Were you baptized into the name of Paul?" (1 Corinthians 1:11-13 New International Version).

You would think that in 1950 years or so Christians would have learned. But now one person says, "I'm a Catholic"; another, "I'm Methodist"; another, "I'm a Baptist"; another, "I'm Presbyterian"; another, "I'm Congregational"; still others are of a multitude of other denominations.

All these denominations put up barriers that dictate what is right and wrong; the sad part about that is that sometimes both the right and the wrong are declared right in the Gospels. Now, allow me to clarify that a little. Sometimes they will say that something Jesus said was right is wrong and things that Jesus said was wrong they say is right. And they always put limits on how far you can go with the Word of God. Now, I'm not talking about what the Bible calls sin but I am talking about what people call sin.

For example, did you know that there are certain denominations that say that speaking in an unknown tongue is of he devil? Many denominations have the mistaken idea that when you confess Jesus as Lord you are automatically filled with the Holy Spirit and you are saved forever, got your *never fading* ticket to heaven and you cannot loose it; can't even throw it away. But no one can give any Bible Scripture to back that up. There's a good reason why they can't, and that is because there aren't any; not unless they are taken way out of context.

People also say that they are new creations in Christ Jesus, but then they say that they are still sinners. That's a religious denominational flaw because if someone is a new creation then the old sinner is dead.

If you will use the 'thinker' that God gave you at His will then you can easily deduce that the very word **denomination** speaks of division. I could take the word and give definitions and synonyms, but I'll purposely let you do that. But some of you don't want to do that.

I have been to many denominational churches; even one called a non-denominational church (it was just another denomination) and I noticed, by the Spirit and by talking to the people, that they don't believe everything that Jesus is.

Many of these denominations believe that only Jesus could do what He did because He was God. Then I would show them this Scripture,

> "Let this same attitude and purpose and [humble] mind be in you which was in Christ Jesus: [Let Him be your example in humility:] Who, although being essentially one with God and in the form of God [possessing the fullness of the attributes which make God God], did not think this equality with God was a thing to be eagerly grasped or retained, But stripped Himself [of all privileges and rightful dignity], so as to assume the guise of a servant (slave), in that He became like men and was born a human being," (Philippians 2:5-7 Amplified Bible).

> "And being found in fashion as a man, he humbled himself, and became obedient unto death, even the

death of the cross," (Philippians 2:8 King James Version).

And they just don't believe it because that's talking about Jesus doing these things as a man anointed with the Holy Spirit. They wanted to believe that they couldn't to these things; such as laying hands on the sick for recovery, casting out demons in His name, speaking in other tongues; the things that Jesus did (John 14:12). They could do those things also if they were anointed-baptized in the Holy Spirit, in God.

What this all comes down to is: Do you want to honor God or your limited denomination?

You do not have to do what I did; but this is what I did. I divorced denominations and denominationalism, because what I was dealing with when I was under denominational rule was a spirit of religions or complacency. That doesn't mean that I don't go to church, I do. It is written,

"Not forsaking the assembling of ourselves together, as the manner of some is; but exhorting one another: and so much the more, as ye see the day approaching," (Hebrews 10:25 King James Version).

In other words, this means do not forsake the assembly of God's people. And since that is where they are, that is where I go. But I don't take part in their denominational stuff. I would rather honor God than any denomination. If you found a way that you can honor God and stay denominational, have at it.

Religions

There is only one true religion. I'm sure some people will look at that statement and think, '*Sure, it's called being a Christian.*' That's an idea that has been taught by many local churches; but it's also a false idea. No. True religion is not being a Christian as many people think.

> "Pure religion and undefiled before God and the Father is this, To visit the fatherless and widows in their affliction, and to keep himself unspotted from the world." (James 1:27 King James Version)

This is true religion. I don't see anything in there about being anything; do you? The world might call you a religious fanatic or something like that because you claim Jesus as Lord, but that's the world. They have sections for religious books, religious music, religious movies and more, but that's how the world views Jesus; as a religious mogul. So, what? That's the world.

In truth, religious groups seem to be filled with traditions and rituals. The dumb thing about that is that these traditions and rituals are not started by God, they are started by man. Then the saying came to life, "We have always done it this way." And when asked why they had always done it that way the religious people would just say, "We don't know, but this is the way our forefathers had always done it." Doesn't that, kind of, remind you of, "This is the way we wash our clothes..."?

109

Then some 'unsmart' person finds a Bible and reads that what his 'religious' church is doing is diametrically opposed to what Jesus taught. So, he brings this news to the attention of his pastor, and subsequently gets booted out of the church.

That pastor, or padre, was not willing to change just because Jesus, God in a human body, said it. That is the epitome of 'religious' churches. The word **complacency** speaks of being self-righteous, smug, self-satisfied, and gratified. When someone looks at you with a smug attitude (you can see it on their face sometimes), they are thinking, '*I'm better than you, fool.*' The Pharisees were self-righteous; this Scripture is a great example,

> "The Pharisee stood and prayed thus with himself, God, I thank thee, that I am not as other men are, extortioners, unjust, adulterers, or even as this publican. I fast twice in the week, I give tithes of all that I possess," (Luke 18:11-12 King James Version).

Satisfaction says that you have the best and there is nothing better; whereas, **contentment** says that you can be happy with what you have but there is something better. Many years ago when I had a Renault automobile a lady in my fellowship group told me that I should be satisfied. Well, it was a good car, but as cars go, it wasn't the best. I had to tell her that I was content but not satisfied.

We can only be satisfied in one fact, one person, one truth; that is that Jesus is Lord and there is no one higher than the almighty God, and the Holy Spirit is the best friend and guide that we could ever have. If you have Jesus as your Lord, you do what He said and did—says and does—and you are baptized in the Holy Spirit and are going to heaven, *and* you are honoring God according to your convictions— the truth—with Jesus and the Holy Spirit then you can be satisfied in that truth.

Now, is there anything else that a Christian church can be satisfied with? I really don't think so. I you can think of something else that you can be satisfied with, as an earthly church, talk to God about it, and maybe talk about it in a discussion group.

Heaven is way better than anything on Earth and the godhead is way better than any preacher or teacher or leader on Earth. The devil is worse than anything, so forget him/it.

"for we walk by faith, not by sight — yet we are confident and satisfied to be out of the body and at home with the Lord," (2 Corinthians 2:7-8 Holman Christian Standard Bible) read the verses around these.

"And the soldiers likewise demanded of him, saying, And what shall we do? And he said unto them, Do violence to no man, neither accuse any falsely; and be content with your wages," (Luke 3:14 King James Version).

Appendix A

Honor = respect, reputation

The scepter will not depart from Judah, nor the
ruler's staff from his descendants, until the
coming of the one to whom it belongs, the one
whom all nations will **honor**.
Genesis 49:10 New Living Translation.

After this presentation to Israel's leaders, Moses
and Aaron went and spoke to Pharaoh. They
told him, "This is what the Lord, the God of
Israel, says: Let my people go so they may hold
a festival in my **honor** in the wilderness."
Exodus 5:1 New Living Translation.

Then Moses said to Aaron, This is what the
Lord meant when He said, I [and My will, not
their own] will be acknowledged as hallowed by
those who come near Me, and before all the
people I will be **honor**ed. And Aaron said
nothing.

113

But the LORD said to Moses and Aaron,
"Because you did not trust in me enough to
honor me as holy in the sight of the Israelites,
you will not bring this community into the land I
give them."
Numbers 20:12 New International Version.

Rather, you must seek the Lord your God at the
place of worship he himself will choose from
among all the tribes—the place where his name
will be **honor**ed.
Deuteronomy 12:5 New Living Translation.

For when the Canaanites and all the other
people living in the land hear about it, they will
surround us and wipe our name off the face of
the earth. And then what will happen to the
honor of your great name?
Joshua 7:9 New Living Translation.

Therefore Jehovah, the God of Israel, saith, I
said indeed that thy house, and the house of thy
father, should walk before me for ever: but now
Jehovah saith, Be it far from me; for them that
honor me I will **honor**, and they that despise me
shall be lightly esteemed.
1 Samuel 2:30 American Standard Version.

And may your name be **honor**ed forever so that
everyone will say, 'The Lord of Heaven's
Armies is God over Israel!' And may the house

of your servant David continue before you
forever.
2 Samuel 7:26 New Living Translation.

But the Lord told him, 'You wanted to build the
Temple to **honor** my name. Your intention is
good,
1 Kings 8:18 New Living Version.

I will add fifteen years to your life, and I will
rescue you and this city from the king of
Assyria. I will defend this city for my own
honor and for the sake of my servant David
2 Kings 20:6 New Livings Translation.

My son, I wanted to build a Temple to **honor**
the name of the Lord my God," David told him
1 Chronicles 22:7 New Living Translation.

Solomon decided to build a Temple to **honor**
the name of the Lord, and also a royal palace for
himself.
2 Chronicles 2:1 New Living Translation.

There are many, many more, but you can look
them up.

Appendix B

Love = worship or align (truly loving God includes obedience because of honor and trust)

When Seth grew up, he had a son and named him Enosh. At that time people first began to **worship** the Lord by name
Genesis 4:26 New Living Translation.

And God said, "I will be with you. And this will be the sign to you that it is I who have sent you: When you have brought the people out of Egypt, you will **worship** God on this mountain."
Exodus 3:12 New International Version

I myself will turn against them and their families and will cut them off from the community. This will happen to all who commit spiritual prostitution by **worship**ing Molech.
Leviticus 20:5 New Living Translations.

So Moses told Israel's judges, "Kill each of the men who **aligned** themselves with Baal of Peor."
Numbers 25:5 Holman Christian Standard Bible

Beware lest you become corrupt by making for yourselves [to **worship**] a graven image in the form of any figure, the likeness of male or female,
Deuteronomy 4:16 Amplified Bible.

If you break the covenant of the LORD your God, which He commanded you, and go and **worship** other gods, and bow down to them, the LORD's anger will burn against you, and you will quickly disappear from this good land He has given you."
Joshua 23:16 Holman Christian Standard Bible.

When Gideon heard the dream and its interpretation, he bowed down and **worship**ed. He returned to the camp of Israel and called out, "Get up! The LORD has given the Midianite camp into your hands."
Judges 7:15 New International Version.

And they rose up in the morning early, and **worship**ped before Jehovah, and returned, and came to their house to Ramah: and Elkanah knew Hannah his wife; and Jehovah remembered her.
1 Samuel 19 American Standard Version.

Then David got up from the ground. After he had washed, put on lotions and changed his clothes, he went into the house of the LORD and **worship**ed. Then he went to his own house, and at his request they served him food, and he ate.
2 Samuel 12:20 New International Version.

Also, the royal officials have come to congratulate our lord King David, saying, 'May your God make Solomon's name more famous than yours and his throne greater than yours!' And the king bowed in **worship** on his bed
1 Kings 1:47 New International Version.

In this thing Jehovah pardon thy servant: when my master goeth into the house of Rimmon to **worship** there, and he leaneth on my hand, and I bow myself in the house of Rimmon, when I bow myself in the house of Rimmon, Jehovah pardon thy servant in this thing.
2 Kings 5:18 American Standard Version.

Ascribe to the Lord the glory due His name. Bring an offering and come before Him; **worship** the Lord in the beauty of holiness and in holy array.
1 Chronicles 16:29 Amplified Bible.

But who is able to build Him a house, since heaven, even highest heaven, cannot contain Him? Who am I to build Him a house, except as a place to burn incense in **worship** before Him?

119

There are many, many more, but you can look them up.

One final question:
Do you want to honor and love God in truth?

Think about it.

www.ingramcontent.com/pod-product-compliance
Lightning Source LLC
Chambersburg PA
CBHW060520030426
42337CB00015B/1956